Tom Brady

The Inspirational Story of Football Superstar Tom Brady

D1057115

presentation of the information is without contract or any type of guarantee assurance.

The trademarks that are used are without any consent, and the publication of the trademark is without permission or backing by the trademark owner. All trademarks and brands within this book are for clarifying purposes only and are the owned by the owners themselves, not affiliated with this document.

Table of Contents

Introduction

As the title implies, this is a short book about [The Inspirational Story of Football Superstar Tom Brady] and how he rose from his life in the San Mateo area to become one of today's leading and most-respected football players. In his rise to superstardom, Tom Brady has inspired not only the youth, but fans of all ages throughout the world.

This book also portrays the struggles Tom had to overcome during his early childhood years, his teen years, until he became what he is today. A notable source of inspiration is Brady's own charitable acts and his consistent support of organizations, such as the Boys and Girls Foundation and numerous others. He continues to serve as the humble, mild-mannered superstar in a sport that glorifies flashy plays and mega personalities.

Combining incredible accuracy, quick decision-making, nimble feet, and superior coordination, he has shown the ability to slice up nearly any defense. From being a slow, non-athletic kid to becoming one of the greatest quarterbacks of all-time, you'll learn how this man has risen to the ranks of the best football players, today.

Although Tom Brady is now one of the best quarterbacks in the National Football League, his rise did not happen overnight. He experienced rejection often, which ultimately, helped him build character and the work ethic needed to succeed. His story is a perfect example of how determination and personal-will can take someone to the top.

Thanks again for grabbing this book. I hope you can take lessons from Tom's life and apply them to your own life!

Chapter 1:

Early Childhood and Youth

Thomas Edward Patrick Brady Jr.'s childhood was filled with football memories. His parents, Galynn and Tom Sr., were huge sports fans, particularly of the San Francisco 49ers. Naturally, it was also the team that young Tom supported, especially because his hometown of San Mateo is just a short drive south of San Francisco. On Sundays, the family would take the 30-minute drive to Candlestick Park to watch Joe Montana lead the team to victories. Early exits during 49ers home games were rare, because the 49ers were a dominant team during that era. The magic of the Bay Area's NFL team captured young Tom, and he had dreams of being in the same position as Montana someday.

He was such a fan, he even cried when his parents did not buy him a 49ers' foam hand. He was also present when Joe Montana threw the desperation pass caught by Dwight Clark, with time running out, to defeat the Dallas Cowboys in the 1981 NFC

Championship Game. That play is forever known as "The Catch", and it would catch a lifelong fan in Brady. However, the physical attributes, evident with athletic kids, were not evident with Tom. Yet, his competitive nature and determination was strong at a young age, thanks to the traits instilled in him by his parents and his three older sisters, Maureen, Julie, and Nancy.

Tom wasn't the biggest or strongest kid on the block, but he did not back down from a physical competition. Sometimes he would challenge the fastest child in the neighborhood, and he would repeatedly suffer defeat. His sister once said in an interview that Tom was smaller than most kids in his neighborhood, but that never stopped him from wanting to play football. Because of his smaller frame, the older kids would mess with him and would tell him to "go long". Tom kept on "going long" until he was tired and haggard, but they never passed the ball to him. However, he used these setbacks as motivation to defeat the odds. He channeled his intelligence and fighting spirit to conquer any challenge thrown at him. He would initially excel in baseball as a catcher, with throwing, hitting, and running skills. It wasn't until his high school days that he played organized American football.

Tom made the varsity football team at the all-boys Junipero Serra High School in San Mateo, California, but was initially slotted as the back-up quarterback. During Tom's 4-year football career with Junipero Serra High, they never made the playoffs. This did not stop him from working hard, especially during training and practice sessions. He knew his opportunity to play would come, and that moment came when the school's starting quarterback suffered an injury, and Tom got his first taste of playing competitive football.

It wasn't until his third year of high school that Tom was officially named the team's starting quarterback. Aside from that, he was also starting on the school's baseball team. Despite the pressure that came with playing two sports, he would continually improve his performance during and after games. He introduced his own jump rope routine, because he deemed the team's current training regimen inefficient. Eventually, his routine became a staple during practices, but he took it even further in the off-season. Every summer, he would initiate a highly physical training program, wherein a selected number of his teammates would join him to work out.

His efforts paid off during his senior season, when he garnered All-State and All-Far West distinctions. Prep Football Report and Blue Chip Illustrated also named him to the All-American squad. At the end of his high school football tenure, Tom totaled 31 touchdown passes and 3,702 passing yards. By the looks of it, he was destined to continue playing football at the collegiate level. However, he also excelled in baseball, so a Major League Baseball team believed he was ready to play for pay right out of high school.

In the 18th round of the 1995 Major League Baseball draft, the Montreal Expos drafted Tom Brady, due to his skills as a hitter and a catcher. He was picked one full round ahead of Aaron Miles and David Ross. The Montreal Expos were asking him to come hit a few balls with them at practice, but he never went. On the flip side, several colleges were trying to recruit Tom into their football programs. He was at a crossroads, but eventually chose football. Down the road, it became a wise decision, as two players drafted by the Expos before him became the team's designated catchers, which was what he was best at playing. With professional baseball out of the equation, Tom had to select a school to play collegiate football. Even though he caught the attention of several colleges near his hometown, he chose to be a Wolverine and suit up for the University of Michigan as a student-athlete.

Chapter 2:

School Career

Just like in high school, Tom was not immediately named the starter for the University of Michigan Wolverines' football team. This was no insult to his talent, but a by-product of having equally talented quarterbacks on the team's roster. There was also a coaching change in Ann Arbor, when Lloyd Carr replaced Gary Moeller. Scott Dreisbach and Brian Griese became the team's top two quarterbacks, while Brady was a red-shirt freshman, which meant he could attend classes at the University, but he could not compete in any school football games. With Brady on the sidelines, the Wolverines tallied a 9-3 win-loss record, but their season ended with an Alamo Bowl loss to the Texas A&M Aggies.

By his sophomore year, Tom was named the team's third-string quarterback. Though this was a major improvement from his status the previous year, he still needed luck to get on the field. He received playing time early on, but it only came when the games were out of reach and the level of competition dropped dramatically, due to the coaches trying to prevent injuries to their star players.

However, Tom would take his time to learn more about the playbook and take practice snaps with the starting players during practice to improve. Overall, the Wolverines were coming back to prominence, thanks to their stellar additions on defense and the heads-up play of Scott Dreisbach, who won the starting quarterback position against Griese. Somehow, the University of Michigan limped its way to the Outback Bowl and defeated Auburn, with Griese named as the starter. This coaching decision confused several people and led to speculations that the starting quarterback position for the upcoming season would be up for grabs. Whether or not Tom thought it was up for grabs, he prepared harder than ever.

Tom would mightily compete for the starting quarterback position in his junior year. However, Griese was, once again, named the official starter, and Brady was named as the third quarterback on the depth chart. Sensing he might miss his opportunity to contribute to a college program, Tom contemplated transferring to the University of California-Berkeley to gain more playing time and possibly a starting role with the team.

His patience eventually won him over, and he stayed with the team, which had all the pieces to win the National Championship. Unfortunately, Brady wouldn't be an active part of the Wolverines' run to the title, as he underwent an appendectomy. He was still recovering from the operation when his team won against Washington State in the Rose Bowl to clinch a share of the National Title.

In his fourth year, Tom set his sights on becoming the starting quarterback, and everything finally seemed to go his way. The countless hours he spent improving his game and learning the team's system paid off, as he was named the starting quarterback after a grueling competition with Dreisbach and the sensational rookie, Drew Henson. Brady struggled early on during his first season as a starter and lost his first two games. However, the team would find valuable chemistry through the struggle and, eventually, improve their record to 2-2.

Then, the most exciting game of the season was next: a game against their bitter rival, the Ohio State Buckeyes. Tom compiled great stats of 375 passing yards and one touchdown pass on 31 completions. However, the team lost by a score of 31-16. After that disappointing game, Brady would assert his leadership on the team, leading them to a ten-game winning streak en route to a Citrus Bowl victory against Arkansas. At year's end, Tom compiled 2,636 passing yards and 15 total touchdown passes. With performances and statistics such as these, it seemed his second season as a starter would be guaranteed.

However, one person gave him a run for his position: the sensational Drew Henson; Henson entered the University with a great deal of hype coming out of high school. Just like Brady in his high school days, Henson was also a two-sport athlete, who was good enough to have a professional career in both. Before joining the Wolverines for his sophomore season, he was drafted by the New York Yankees and played Class-A professional baseball. Sports experts and coaches marked Henson as a once-in-a-generation player, who could beat Brady for the starting job. Yet, the ever-reliable Brady lived up to the challenge. Coach Carr had a hard time choosing a starter for their season opener against Notre Dame. Eventually, he gave both quarterbacks playing time during the game.

During the initial stages of the game, Brady and Henson took turns leading the offense to multiple field goals. Eventually, Carr chose Brady to finish the game. Brady responded impressively with a victory against the Fighting Irish, which led by 14 points. He finished the game with 197 passing yards on 17 completions. Henson was still a threat to Brady's position; however, as the season progressed, Brady was pulling away from Henson in the quarterback contest. He would record stellar performances against Purdue, Michigan State, and Illinois. Carr, eventually, proclaimed Brady as the unanimous starting quarterback.

With his position secured, Brady led the Wolverines to four straight wins to secure a bid in the Orange Bowl against the Alabama Crimson Tide. He would then give his finest performance in college football, as he passed for 369 yards and four touchdowns, including a 25-yard game-winner to Shawn Thompson. The final score of the impressive game was 35-34. His ability to read and dissect defensive schemes enabled Tom to tally 2,586 yards, 20 touchdown passes, and only six interceptions for the entire season. With his college career over, he declared his eligibility for the NFL draft. However, most NFL teams did not regard him highly as a prospect.

Despite his success as quarterback in Michigan, Tom's teammates thought of him as a humble guy, who just loved to play football. No one ever said Tom was flashy or boastful. He had once been a boy with simple dreams. This was evidenced when his teammate, Aaron Shea, asked him what he would do if he made it big in the NFL. The young Tom Brady answered he would like new socks every day. He didn't say he wanted a big house or a brand new, top of the line car. When Shea asked Brady if he was serious, he said he loves new socks. Tom said he dreams of putting on a pair of new socks every day and then throwing them away at the end of the day.

Here's another tidbit you probably didn't know about Tom when he was in college. He worked as an intern for Merrill Lynch. He once posted a copy of his old resume on his social media account, where his experience in banking was listed. He held the position of assistant to a Senior Sales Broker in Merrill Lynch, in Ann Arbor during the summers of 1998 and 1999.

Tom was quoted as saying he thought he might need his resume, implying he needed to look for a new job, when his name wasn't called in the fifth round of the NFL draft in 2000. Had he not been drafted into playing professional football, you can bet he would have been a very successful banker. He earned high grades and built up some work experience, like being a Sales Rep for different golf courses around Michigan.

Chapter 3:

Professional Life

As mentioned, by the time Tom graduated from Michigan, it wasn't certain he would have a professional football career. While his leadership skills were evident with the Wolverines, scouts raised caution over his physical attributes and skills. They pointed out several flaws in his game, particularly his inability to run away from chasing defenders and his perceived struggle to throw the "deep ball". At the NFL Combine, Tom was deemed too skinny to be a professional quarterback by some scouts, and he ran the 40-yard-dash in 5.2 seconds, considered a slow pace. With most of the team officials focusing on his physical attributes, they gave low remarks for him as an NFL prospect.

This translated into a forgettable experience for Tom during the 2000 NFL Draft. Tom was told he would be taken in the first few rounds of the draft. However, as his name was not called until late into the draft,

Tom released his anger by whacking a few items in his parents' backyard with a baseball bat.

Finally, Tom Brady Jr. was taken in the sixth round, as the 199th overall pick. He was the seventh quarterback taken from twelve. The six quarterbacks taken before him and the team they were drafted by were : the New York Jets drafted Chad Pennington of Marshall (1st round, 18th overall), the San Francisco 49ers took Giovanni Carmazzi of Hofstra (3rd round, 65th overall), the Baltimore Ravens selected Chris Redman of Louisville (3rd round, 75th overall), the Pittsburgh Steelers acquired Tee Martin of Tennessee (5th round, 163rd overall), the New Orleans Saints picked Mark Bulger of West Virginia (6th round, 168th overall), and the Cleveland Browns chose Spergon Wynn of Southwest Texas State (6th round, 183rd overall).

Later, reports surfaced that the Patriots considered getting Tim Rattay, instead of Tom, as their draft pick. Despite his low draft position, Tom cracked the New England Patriots' roster as the third string quarterback, behind Drew Bledsoe and John Friesz. Still, a few of his teammates were skeptical regarding why the team drafted him. Day by day, Tom would earn the respect of his Patriots teammates through his determination to learn more about the game and improve his physical stature via weight training.

He would also improve his arm strength and his footwork, but still, gaining playing time seemed to be a distant dream. Drew Bledsoe was the hands-down starter, and no one believed Tom would displace him soon. In his rookie season, Tom had one pass completion, out of three attempts, for six yards. However, he would be announced as the team's number two quarterback before the start of the 2001 NFL season. Just like his time at Michigan, Tom was moving up in the depth charts, slowly, but surely.

Even though he was now the heir apparent, there was still no indication he would equal or surpass the talent of Bledsoe. While the Patriots lost their 2001 season opener to the Cincinnati Bengals, it was not enough for a quarterback change. However, as fate would have it, the second game of the same season became a defining one for Brady and the entire Patriots organization.

In a game against the New York Jets, Drew Bledsoe was running to the sidelines and was ferociously bumped by linebacker, Mo Lewis, as he was about to step out of bounds. Bledsoe suffered a career-threatening, sheared blood vessel, but he could still go back into the game. Eventually, Patriots head coach, Bill Belichick, had Brady finish the game, which ended in another defeat with a score of 10-3.

After the game, Drew Bledsoe would be ruled out by the team for at least the next few games of the season.

With Bledsoe out because of the injury, Brady was named the team's starter. However, his personal success did not come immediately, as he struggled mightily in his first two games as the starter by posting quarterback ratings of below 80. Despite the low ratings, the team would split these two games with a victory over the Indianapolis Colts and a loss to the Miami Dolphins. Tom's breakout game came against the San Diego Chargers, when they were trailing by ten points, well into the fourth quarter.

In dramatic fashion, Tom led his team to tie the game and force overtime. The Patriots won the game, and Brady completed 33 passes for 364 yards, with two passing touchdowns. In the next game, Brady led the Patriots to a thrashing of the Indianapolis Colts, with a score of 38-17. Eventually, Tom garnered an 11-3 record as a starter, and the Patriots were on their way to the NFL Playoffs. Tom would compile 2,843 passing yards, 18 touchdowns, and an invitation to the Pro Bowl!

The New England Patriots earned a first round playoff bye and faced the Oakland Raiders in the

AFC Divisional Playoff round. With a few minutes left in the game, the Raiders were leading by three, when Tom Brady acted to pass and former Michigan teammate, Charles Woodson, knocked the ball out of his hands. The Raiders recovered the ball, but referee Walt Coleman employed the tuck rule; wherein, the play was ruled as an incomplete pass and not a fumble. The Patriots kept possession and won the game, as Brady threw for 312 yards. One week later, he started the AFC Championship Game against the Pittsburgh Steelers, but injured his knee. Drew Bledsoe, who had recovered from his injury, took over and won the game to clinch a Super Bowl berth against the heavily favored St. Louis Rams.

Leading into the Super Bowl, it was predicted the Rams would decimate the Patriots, due to the Ram's high-octane offense, nicknamed "The Greatest Show on Turf". Even odds makers in Las Vegas placed New England as a 14-point underdog. Aside from this proclaimed mismatch, Belichick had a dilemma, regarding whether to start Bledsoe or Brady in the most important game of the season. The support of the locker room was with Brady, mainly because the opportunity to play for the championship would not have been possible without him. Belichick heeded to their sentiments, as Brady started and played the entire game.

With a masterful game plan by the entire Patriots' coaching staff and a physical defense that threw the Rams' players from their timing, the game was close. Even though the Patriots once had a 14-point lead, it was easily erased by the Rams' offense. With the game tied at 17 with 1:51 left, Brady led his team from their own side of the field into the Ram's territory. A field goal by Adam Vinatieri sealed the game for the Patriots, and Brady became the youngest quarterback to win a Super Bowl. From a sixth-round draft pick and a third-string quarterback, Tom reached the top of the football world, and he was named Super Bowl MVP as the cherry on top. On a sad note, Bledsoe lost his job for good, and Brady has not relinquished his position to anyone since then.

Despite Brady's early success, the Patriots could not repeat as champions the next season. The Patriots posted a 9-7 record in Tom's second season as the starter, and they failed to make the playoffs. However, all of their frustrations were channeled into the next season, as Tom led the Patriots to a 14-2 record and another Super Bowl victory against the Carolina Panthers. Tom would finish the season with 3,620 passing yards and 23 touchdowns. In the season following the second Super Bowl, the team would repeat as champions by winning against the Philadelphia Eagles in Super Bowl XXXIX, with a score of 24-21. Brady finished the regular season with 3,692 passing yards and 28 touchdowns.

After their third Super Bowl win, Brady led the Patriots to the postseason in all, but one, season. The missing year was 2008, and it was due to the hit by Kansas City Chiefs safety, Bernard Pollard, which caused Brady to tear his anterior cruciate ligament (ACL) and medial collateral ligament (MCL). In 2007, Brady led his team to a perfect regular season record of 16-0, and they were at 18-0 going into the Super Bowl. Unfortunately, they were defeated in the big game by the New York Giants, 17-14, on a touchdown pass from Eli Manning to Plaxico Burress, with 35 seconds left in the game.

As a football player, Tom is known in the NFL for his competitive nature. His teammates and everyone else within the New England Patriots organization and staff know he dislikes losing. He has argued with referees and teammates over bad calls and plays. His father was once quoted, saying Tom's competitive attitude started at age 4 and was fully realized by age 8. He loves to win all his games, even charity games. At one charity game in 2009, Tom barked at his teammates for not giving their entire effort to the game.

Tom also doesn't like to miss a game or a practice session. The backup quarterbacks on the Patriots roster rarely had playtime, while Tom was playing.

Despite this, they still feel Tom is an inspiration, and they are happy to play with him. During the 2005 season, Tom played with an enlarged pair of testicles, which resulted from a sports hernia. His dedication to the game really showed when he played hard throughout the campaign, despite his injury.

Another inspirational thing about Tom as a player is that he appreciates squad players who can pick him off. He doesn't act like a superstar or a big shot football star, getting mad at players who tackle him, like some other stars of his stature. He prefers to make himself a better player, and instead, tries to improve his runs and throws to outmaneuver the tacklers and interceptions.

Tom works hard to make sure he's always on top of his game. He goes to the gym bright and early and spends countless hours working out. He has an early bedtime (at around 8:30-9PM!) and rarely goes to parties and clubs. He reportedly took a nap before his first Super Bowl and woke up 30 minutes before kickoff. Talk about power napping!

He maintains this schedule, even during the off-season. He has completed the required football drills through the end of the season, even if his team didn't make it to the final game. His discipline earned him several awards, including multiple league MVP and Super Bowl MVP awards.

Tom had become close to the owner of the Patriots, Robert Kraft. He once introduced himself to him, and the billionaire replied saying, "I know who you are, Tom Brady. You're our sixth round draft choice". Not fazed by the owner's blatant comment, Tom replied with a great comeback, saying he's the best decision the team ever made. This later proved to be prophetic.

Tom is close to many of his teammates, not just the coaching staff and management. He reportedly calls his teammates "babe", which is a term of endearment, normally used by lovers. According to his teammates, this is his way of making you feel at ease in one of the most cutthroat professions in the world. Tom once gave his team and the staff of the Patriots UGGs, a product he endorses.

Chapter 4:

Personal Adult Life

Fans know Tom Brady as one of the best quarterbacks of all-time. However, to people who are not really football fans, they know him as a handsome man with a beautiful, wealthy wife, who is one of the top supermodels in the world. Some people would be jealous and others envious of that. But Tom is not a cocky guy, by any means.

He keeps his personal life out of the public eye, unless asked about it, and he doesn't brag about any of his past accomplishments, even though very few players will ever reach those types of accolades. He maintains a friendly and generous attitude when asked to give analyses of opposing players. He has no problem complementing other great players, like Peyton Manning, or up-and-coming stars, like Russell Wilson. He doesn't seem to feel threatened by the greatness of other players, but thrives in the competitive nature of trying to be the best he can be.

He has been a humble and giving superstar his entire career, probably because he's never had it easy on any level of football. He's always had to work hard to secure his spot on a team, and he knows what hard work means. He takes nothing for granted, either. You won't find Tom starting brawls or acting crazy in bars. He rarely drinks, doesn't do drugs, or anything that could harm his career in any way. Instead of going out to parties after every win, he prefers to stay at home and take a good night's rest. He knows he always needs to be on top of his game, and good habits have made him a great player.

Tom met his wife, Gisele Bundchen, on a blind date set up by a common friend. Gisele later said in an interview that when she met Tom, it was love at first sight. She was quoted saying, "I could see it in his eyes that he was a man with integrity who believes in the same things I do". Gisele proved to be a gem for sticking it out with Tom, after the news had surfaced that he got ex-girlfriend, Moynahan, pregnant soon after their first date. They both found it very challenging, at first, but it also strengthened their bond. Gisele was also quoted saying this event made her see the man Tom is. It showed her his integrity and highlighted what a good person Tom really is. This endeared him even more to the Brazilian supermodel.

Gisele and Tom soon became a household item. They would be photographed often on hundreds of occasions and events that required their appearance. They tried to keep out of the paparazzi's eyes as much as possible and spent most of their time together in private. Both Gisele and Tom had a thing for keeping their relationship private, rather than putting on a drama filled show for their fans and critics. They were certainly the "it" couple, when they were dating.

It didn't seem to matter to Tom that his girlfriend was one of the highest paid models, and her paycheck outweighed his by a margin. Tom was confident about his love for Gisele and vice versa. Things like this didn't seem to matter. Gisele was also the most sought after model during the time she and Tom dated. She was a Victoria's secret supermodel and a highly in demand product endorser.

Despite the hectic schedule, she and Tom made it work. Their relationship flourished, and they were married on February 26th, 2009. They have been together since then and have two children, Benjamin Rein and Vivian Lake. The couple owns homes in Beverly Hills, Manhattan, and Boston. Meanwhile, Tom's sister, Julie, is married to Red Sox legend, Kevin Youkilis.

Tom is known by his family and friends as a great family man. When he is not playing football, he can be found at home with his family. He would lovingly post photos of him and his wife, or him and his children on his social media accounts. He and Gisele have also been photographed often playing and spending time with their children. They go on trips to the beach, to amusement parks, and do fun activities, like running around in a scooter with the kids.

Tom is also a highly sought after product endorser with current endorsements for Dodge, Under Armour, and UGGS. He also had endorsement deals with Got Milk?, Wheaties, and Movado. He has also graced several magazine covers, including ESPN: The Magazine, Sports Illustrated, Men's Health, Esquire, Best Life, Details, Vogue, and GQ. He has also guest stared on Saturday Night Live, and he included himself in one episode of The Simpsons and an episode of Family Guy.

Tom also has several interests outside of football. To his family and friends, he is a very serious ping pong player. He reportedly has a ping pong paddle that looks worn out and beat up from countless use. Needless to say, his competitiveness transfers into any sport or game that he picks up.

Tom, just like any other guy, has his own quirks and unusual habits. There have been reports saying Tom keeps coconut water in his locker, and he likes to snack on avocado flavored ice cream. His mother also said he likes hummus.

As part of his healthy regimen, Tom eats organic fruits and vegetables, reportedly grown in his own backyard. He also has a very strict exercise regimen to keep his physique and explosiveness in top shape. An article in Sports Illustrated revealed Tom has everything calculated and planned, so he can play until he is 48 years old. He does cognitive exercises to wind down at night, and as mentioned in the previous chapter, he sleeps early. Tom also has a brain resiliency program, wherein a workout was made especially for his brain to help him process information quicker, improve his memory, and increase his peripheral vision.

When he is not with his wife and kids, Tom is mostly focused on playing football and improving his game. His dedication and advance planning has enabled him to become one of football's greatest quarterbacks.

Chapter 5:

Philanthropic and Charitable Acts

Throughout his career, Tom has supported several charities. He is most commonly associated with Best Buddies International, which aims to provide people with intellectual disabilities with employment opportunities and one-on-one friendships. Tom is an avid supporter of the group. He often hosts events for them and campaigns for their causes as much as he can. He joins the sports-related programs set by Best Buddies International and promotes their causes, personally. His appearance at the organization's events has greatly increased awareness and support for the cause.

Tom also supports the Boys and Girls Club of America, which provides after school programs for the youth. It was founded in 1860 and now has a nationwide reach. In an interview for the charity, Tom said he believes in the causes the Boys and Girls Club of America are advocating, because he is a parent and can identify with the need to provide children with worthy after school programs. Tom was named an honorary chair in 2012 when the Boys and Girls Club of America joined the Rodman Ride For Kids fundraising event.

Another cause that Tom supports is the Entertainment Industry Foundation. Though Tom is a professional athlete and has no ties to the entertainment world, other than being married to a supermodel, he is still considered by the Entertainment Industry Foundation to be a great role model and a powerful voice that can reach thousands of people. So they tapped him, along with other famous sports superstars and celebrities, to raise funds for various charities that the foundation supports.

KaBOOM! is another cause that Tom supports. Just like the Boys and Girls Club of America, KaBOOM! is a non-profit organization that focuses on developing worthy activities for kids. It aims to bring active play as part of a child's daily activity and, particularly, focuses on children who live in poverty-stricken areas. They create places within the community where children can play and be active in sports, among other things.

Tom supports the Active Force Foundation, which focuses on designing and developing sports equipment that individuals who are physically challenged can use to have an active life. He believes in giving everyone, even those with physical challenges, a chance to enjoy an active lifestyle. Tom knows the value of good sports equipment, as he too relies on them to help him improve his game. He wants everyone to achieve their dreams of becoming the best athlete that they can - even if they never make a career out of it.

Tom is also involved with the Starlight Children's Foundation of New England, which helps ill children and their families cope with fear through educational and entertaining activities. The Starlight Children's Foundation partners with several hospitals and clinics and enables them to forward their needs to the foundation to get funding. They operate in several countries worldwide and have helped thousands of families during their time of need.

Tom has also embarked on an eight-day trip to Ghana and Uganda, courtesy of One.org and the Debt AIDS Trade Africa. There, he visited clinics and schools. Tom said it was his first trip to Africa. Since his trip, he has been actively lobbying for an increase in the humanitarian aid budget to help Africans increase their quality of life. Tom has been one of One.org's most influential supporters and has been a leader in spreading word about its causes.

From this list alone, you see Tom Brady knows how to give back. He's been using his success in football and overall fame to advocate for causes that benefit children, the physically challenged, and the poor. He uses his social media to campaign for his causes and encourage his supporters to help. He also finds time to support these causes in person, despite his rigorous training and balancing his family life. Because of this, many people look up to Tom, not just for his success in football, but also for his generosity and strong character.

Chapter 6:

Legacy and Inspiration for Others

Tom Brady's story reminds us that long-term success does not happen overnight. Working hard and working smart always comes before achievements, and this is especially evident in his journey. Although he has been deemed an underdog at times, he continued to work towards excellence. Eventually, others noticed his potential because of the dedication he placed into his chosen profession.

When looking from a macro scale, it is evident that Tom's career is worthy of the Hall of Fame. He's already won more sporting awards than most fans can count; yet, he remains humble and dedicated to improving his game. He has broken several football records and is aiming to break more in the coming years. He is someone young athletes look up to for inspiration. Children idolize him for his athleticism and intelligence in football and want to be like him when they grow up.

Tom tries his best to live up to his fan's picture of him and takes nothing for granted. He works hard to improve himself and wants to bring his team to more Super Bowls than any player has ever. He knows his hard work will pay off eventually, and believes there is no shortcut to success.

To his fellow athletes, teammates, and competitors, Tom is a force to be reckoned with. He is a beast on the field and an unrelenting opponent. The owners, coaches, and staff of the New England Patriots will always remember Tom as an amazing quarterback and will forever sing his praises for the great things he has done for the team. He is admired not just by young, up and coming athletes, but also revered by sports personalities and great athletes across the globe.

Tom's professional football career is not the only thing he has going for him. He has become a household name and has been thrust into the spotlight, whether or not he likes it. He has fans who are not necessarily football fans, and their numbers are growing by the day. He is admired by people of all ages and has become a celebrity in his own right. He has thousands of followers on his social media accounts, even if he rarely posts activities in his personal life. They admire him for continuing to uphold his privacy in the age of oversharing and immediate gratification.

He remains humble and true to his roots and continues to focus on his football career, rather than deviating to the lure of a more lucrative career as a celebrity. He doesn't endorse products he deems will send a negative message to his young fans. Instead, he promotes a healthy lifestyle and insists discipline and hard work will be tools that will help you succeed in everything you do. He keeps his body healthy, not to look good in photographs, but to stay in top shape during the games. He shares his fitness regimen with his fans and encourages them to get into sports.

Tom's friends admire him for his love for football and his family. They also appreciate the way he finds time for his friends, despite his busy schedule. To his friends, he is a loyal and trustworthy person. He values his friends, just as much as he values his family. He treats them well and has given unexpected presents and surprises that delight them. He considers his trainer, Alex Guerrero, one of his best friends.

Tom also wants to be the family guy his fans can look up to. He wants to be the best father for his children and the best husband for his wife. He knows the value of family, and he wants his fans to see the importance of spending time with them. He only has good words for his family and has not spoken negatively about them in public. He keeps his personal life quiet as much as possible and rarely gives interviews about his family.

He and his supermodel wife, reportedly, kept their engagement and wedding equally private. This was displayed when his wife said in an interview that they were engaged long before news had circulated. He and his family understand that not everything needs to be publicized. He tries to balance his family and football, so he can give his best at both. He tries to immerse himself in all aspects of parenting, despite his crazy schedule. He embraces parenthood and deals with everything a dad must do for his children with a very happy disposition. As his children have grown, Tom has changed his routine to fit into his family life.

Tom's relationship with his parents and siblings is something to be admired. He loves his father and mother dearly and has a good relationship with them. He dotes on his sisters and loves their children like his own. Some athletes forget where they came from once they reach the big leagues, but not Tom. He still finds time to be with his family as much as he can. He also goes back to his old high school and college every once in a while, to talk and to inspire young people. He holds no grudge against those who taunted him in the past and considers them learning experiences. These experiences made him tougher and stronger and helped him reach his goals. He encourages his young fans to do the same, to never give up, and persevere, to fight harder, and be better than they were the day or year before.

Whatever path in life, if a person plans on doing anything significant, there will be doubters along the way and people who will be better, initially. Consider this motivation, not defeat. These are the mountains you have to climb to be victorious. But as you have climbed one mountain, you are more confident in the next one. As we've explored, many people doubted Tom's ability as a quarterback when he was in college and when he was coming into the NFL. However, he made the most of every opportunity and was not pressured by the situation, because he knew how much work he had put in and trusted all of his preparation.

Through all of his struggles, Tom now understands that no matter what he does, he cannot please everybody. He just has to do his best and give it all his effort. He knows people will criticize him and he shouldn't take their criticisms to heart unless he feels the same way. He prefers to focus on things that matter to him, rather than listening to rumors and naysayers. This mindset enables him to block out all the distractions and keep quiet, even if he is being subjected to criticism.

Tom's football and personal career have been watched closely by fans all over the globe. He is admired in several countries, and the whole world knows what a great athlete he is. He plans to continue his legacy as the New England Patriot's best quarterback and has been working hard to make his dreams come true. He reportedly makes 3 year plans and follows his schedule strictly.

Ask anyone who knows Tom and you will only hear good things about him. However, to those who know his competitive spirit, he is sometimes described as tough and could make a grown man cower when he is angry, but that can be attributed to his love for winning, which he never quite outgrew!

Conclusion

Hopefully this book helped you to gain inspiration from the life of Tom Brady, one of the best players in the National Football League.

The rise and fall of a star is often the cause for much wonder. However, most stars have an expiration date. In football, once a star player reaches his mid- to late-thirties, it is often time to contemplate retirement. What will be left in people's minds about that fading star? In Tom Brady's case, people will remember how he led one team in their journey towards the playoffs. He will be remembered as the guy, who plucked his team from obscurity, helped them build their image, and honed his own image, along the way.

Tom has also inspired many people because he is the star who never failed to look back. He has paid his dues forward by helping thousands of less-fortunate youth find their inner light through sports and education, and by helping those less fortunate in other countries increase the quality of their lives.

Another thing that stands out in Tom Brady's history is that he never forgot where he came from. As soon as he could give back, he poured what he had straight back to those who needed it, and he continues to do so to this day.

Hopefully you've learned some great things about Tom in this book and can apply some of the lessons to your own life!

Made in the USA
San Bernardino, CA
03 April 2018